The Colour of Steam

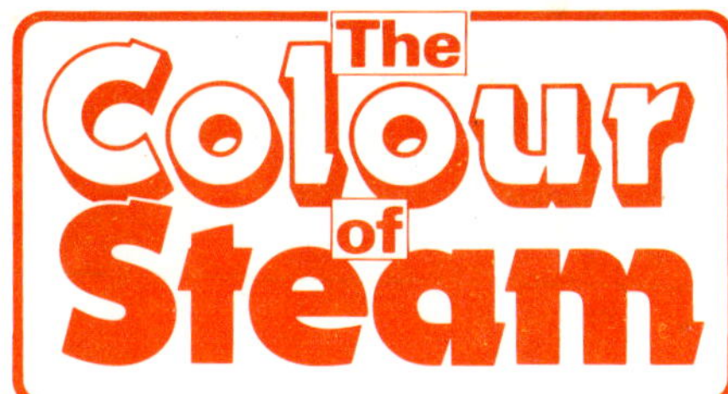

Volume One
GREAT WESTERN MAIN LINES

Editor/Captions
NIGEL TREVENA

Original Photography
R.C. RILEY
M. MENSING
P.M. ALEXANDER
(Millbrook House Collection, courtesy of P.B. Whitehouse)
DEREK CROSS
GEOFFREY BANNISTER
H.G. FORSYTHE
BRIAN MOONE
J.C. MORGAN
JOHN TARRANT

First Published 1984

Designed by Nigel Trevena
Printed by Century Litho, Penryn, Cornwall

ISBN 0 906899 11 7

Published by
ATLANTIC (Transport & Historical) PUBLISHERS 25 Scorrier Street St Day Redruth Cornwall TR16 5LH

Atlantic

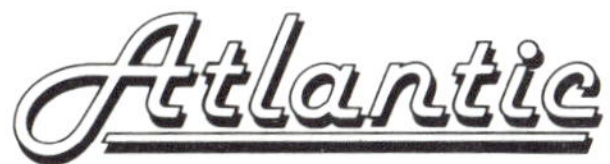

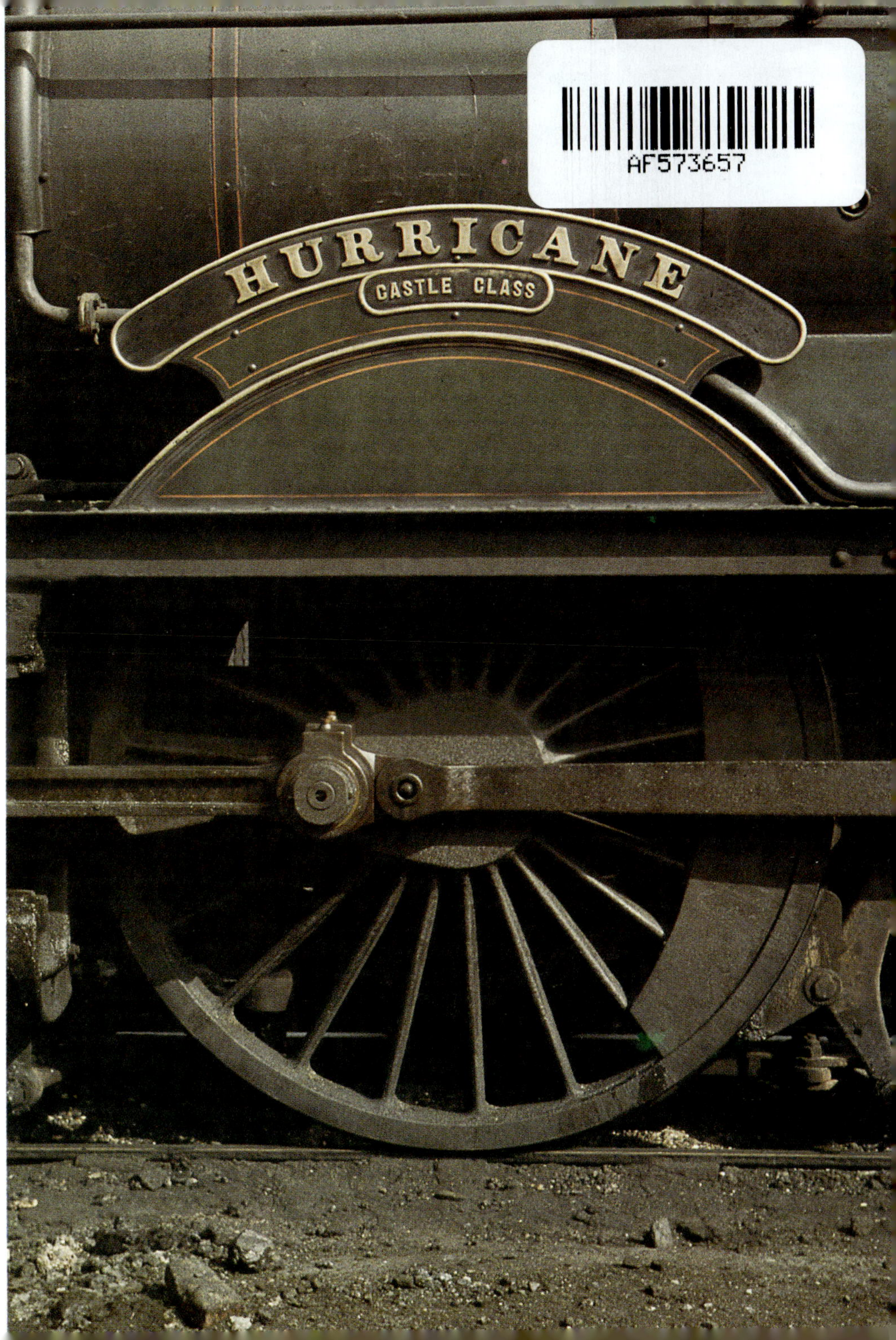

The Western in colour

Colour, it has been said, is a funny thing. Difficult to define, it defies description and, most regrettably, baffles the memory. Yet, without it, a recorded scene is robbed of life. Colour ennobles it, resolves its detail and enhances its value to historian, enthusiast and aesthete alike.

The student of the steam railway has been well provided with published black and white material, but historic photographs in colour have been few and far between: they are scarce, and complicated and expensive to reproduce. In this book, the first in the *Colour of Steam* series, the good offices of some of the finest railway photographers are combined with 'state of the art' laser-based, computer-controlled printing technology to produce a colour record of ex-Great Western main line steam in its last years. The purist may cavill at the BR crest on the locomotives, but, in essence, the scenes are pure Great Western: visually, very little changed in the decade or two after Nationalisation.

A variety of locations, motive power and liveries have been carefully selected: clean engines are here but so are the filthy engines of the last years as they, too, were part of the story. The emphasis, usually, is on the train, but stations, signals, sheds, yards - the railway infrastructure in all its richness - will feature in the *Colour of Steam* series, and *preserved* steam will be specifically excluded.

As a humble purveyor of captions, the writer can only record his indebtedness to those distinguished photographers whose work appears in these pages: who pioneered railway colour photography in an era when colour film was less sophisticated, and the hobby incomparably less popular, than today. They usually did it for fun, but their achievement increases in significance as the years go by. It has been a pleasure to edit their material; a privilege to publish it.

The reader who is seeking the minutiae of the Great Western's operations will need to look elsewhere. In this book, through the incomparable medium of *colour* photography, he will find pictorial reality in its truest form. This is the way it really was.

Nigel Trevena, Series Editor

FRONT COVER: Castle No.5056 *Earl of Powis* emerges from Twerton Tunnel near Bath with a down express in the late 1950's.
Photo: P.M. Alexander/Millbrook House Collection
BACK COVER: No.7812 *Erlestoke Manor* (now preserved on the Severn Valley Railway), heads a Birmingham Snow Hill-Aberystwyth Sunday excursion near closed Middletown station on 23rd August 1964. *Photo: M. Mensing*
TITLE PAGE: Centre driving wheel of Castle No.5072 *Hurricane*, photographed at Cardiff Canton shed in September 1960.
Photo: P.M. Alexander/Millbrook House Collection
THIS PAGE: No.6027 *King Richard I* at King's Sutton with an up Birmingham express, October 1961.
Photo: P.M. Alexander/Millbrook House Collection

The 'right-away'

R. C. Riley **9th April 1960**

St Erth station in the far west of Cornwall. On the footplate of No.4083 *Abbotsbury Castle* Driver Leonard Rail of Penzance shed watches intently as extra vans are added to his train, the 1.30 pm Penzance-York broccoli special. By this date, this was an unusual turn for a Castle, Granges and Halls being the most common motive power for this once heavy perishable traffic.

Visible on the left are the sight feed lubricators, which fed oil under steam pressure to the cylinders, the long regulator handle and the handle of the reversing gear projecting across the cab window. Above these is the bell for the Automatic Train Control system. Great Western engines were, of course, right hand drive and Rail's fireman will shortly be watching for the 'right-away'.

Through the curves

M. Mensing **16th May 1959**

The main line through Cornwall combines a seemingly endless succession of reverse curves with undulating gradients: a severe test for enginemen and locomotives alike. Here, one of the earliest Halls, No.4908 *Blakesley Hall,* approaches Chacewater station on a sunny spring evening with the 5.50 pm Penzance-Truro local. Opened in 1852 by the West Cornwall Railway, Chacewater became junction for the 18-mile branch to Newquay in 1903 and closed on 5th October 1964 following the branch's demise the year before. From 1924, Newquay trains left the station on an independent line parallel to the up main - seen here disappearing behind the engine's smokebox.

A Penzance engine, No.4908 left Cornwall in March 1960 and was withdrawn from Didcot shed in October 1963.

Mixed traffic masters

R. C. Riley **9th July 1961**

Truro - based No.6828 *Trellech Grange* rumbles into Liskeard, junction for the picturesque Looe branch, with the 3.55 pm Tavistock Junction - Falmouth freight. While both the Castle and Hall 4-6-0's performed sterling work in Cornwall for some forty years, the sure-footed, smaller-wheeled Granges proved complete masters of the county's severe banks and for a considerable period were dominant on passenger workings in the Duchy.

On shed at Laira

R. C. Riley **17th July 1960**

The County 4-6-0's were also familiar in Cornwall during the 1950's. This view of Laira shed, Plymouth, shows a visitor from Swindon - No.1010 *County of Caernarvon* beside the coaling stage. Laira shed comprised a 28-road roundhouse dating from 1901 plus a four-road 'straight' shed opened in 1931.

Over the Devon banks

R. C. Riley **29th June 1957**

Veteran Castle No.4088 *Dartmouth Castle*, one of the second batch built 1925, leaves 274-yard Dainton Tunnel with the 8.45 am Liverpool-Penzance. Behind her is the gruelling climb up from Aller Junction on gradients of 1 in 55 and 1 in 37: her fireman can now take a breather on the down grades to Totnes.

On a summer Saturday at this period, this section of main line saw the most intensive express passenger service in Britain, a continuous succession of heavy holiday trains climbing to Dainton Summit from both directions with, at peak periods, only seven or eight minutes headway between them. All manner of 6-coupled engines were pressed into service, including Class 4300 Moguls and 2-8-0's of the 2800 and 4700 Classes, hauling a great variety of sometimes ancient coaching stock, both ex-GWR and from other regions, which was little used during the rest of the year.

All trains grappled with the entirely unwelcome legacy of a line designed for Brunel's atmospheric railway but never so used - the severe gradients, which included, at 1 in 36, the steepest stretch of main line in Britain.

Top-link freight

R. C. Riley **14th July 1959**

When, with characteristic aplomb, I. K. Brunel threw the South Devon Railway along the coast between Exeter and Dawlish, he provided the SDR's successor - the Great Western - with its finest possible showcase, an asset of inestimable benefit in popularising the 'Great Way West'. The first section, from Exeter to Teignmouth, opened to passengers on 30th May 1846 and onwards to Newton Abbot the following year. It was, of course, laid to broad gauge, converted to standard in 1892 and, following a widening of the sea wall, doubled in 1905.

Here, with the summer sky and sea reflecting on her boiler, No.4949 *Packwood Hall* hurries an up fish train at Teignmouth. Once, this type of traffic was of immense importance to the GWR in the West Country; vast tonnages were carried in fully-fitted wagons worked, like all perishable traffic, to 'top-link' standards and schedules. In 1938, more than half originated in one port - Newlyn - only Brixham and Plymouth even approaching the Cornish village in importance. Today, the industry is in decline and traffic, such as it is, goes by road.

Rail, steam and sea

R. C. Riley **3rd July 1957**

Devon had no finer railway spectacle: a headboard-carrying, Great Western 4-6-0 in lined Brunswick Green in full cry by the blue Devon sea. This is Castle No.5059 *Earl St Aldwyn*; the train is the 11.25 am Kingswear-Paddington - 'The Torbay Express', which will run non-stop to Exeter and thence 'fast' to Paddington, one of the few trains at that time not to stop at Newton Abbot. The stock, BR standard Mk.I coaches introduced in 1951, is predominantly in traditional GWR-style chocolate and cream livery, reintroduced by the Western Region in the mid-1950's, although one 'blood and custard' vehicle mars the uniformity of the rake.

Homeward bound

R. C. Riley **23rd June 1962**

One of Penzance's Granges, No.6827 *Llanfrechfa Grange*, departs from Exeter St Davids at 7.30 pm with the 3.50 pm Pylle Hill Sidings-Penzance parcels. She is passing Exeter West signal box, a fine example of a manual box on the grand scale which was made redundant in the 1980's by the establishment of new power boxes at Exeter and Westbury and is, at the time of writing, the subject of a preservation attempt.

Above the box is the link line to the Southern Region's Exeter Central station, opened on 1st February 1862 to enable LSWR trains to run through to the Exeter and Crediton line. The stiff climb up to Central is at 1 in 37 and banking of most trains was once necessary, a duty performed for some twenty years by the Class E1/R 0-6-2T's of LBSC origin. These were replaced by Class M7 tanks, Standard tanks and latterly the massive Class Z 0-8-0T's and Class W 2-6-4T's. 1964 saw the end of steam banking at Exeter, Western 0-6-0PT's performing the last rites.

There were, and still are, six platforms at Exeter St Davids: No.1 (down main); No.2 (bay once used by Exe Valley branch trains); Nos.3&4 (middle island, used by SR trains); Nos.5&6 (island used by WR trains, No.5 being the up main).

Express from the West

R. C. Riley **26th July 1958**

A fine study of a typical ex-GWR halt-style station: Long Sutton & Pitney on the West of England main line in Somerset, just east of Curry Rivell Junction. No.5026 *Criccieth Castle*, from Oxford shed, is running through at speed with the non-stop 11.30 am Torquay-Paddington.

The charming little 'pagoda' shelters in GWR light and dark stone paint were of a type supplied in kit form by an outside contractor and used extensively for a variety of purposes throughout the GWR system. Long Sutton & Pitney was relegated from full station status to unstaffed halt on 26th September 1955 and closed on 10th September 1962.

In the 1950's most West of England expresses carried prominent train reporting numbers as seen here. Large metal characters were affixed to a frame mounted on the locomotive's smokebox door. Introduced by the GWR in 1934, this system was a response to problems in train identification caused by the numerous relief workings and trains running out of booked sequence during peak summer traffic periods. The first of the three numbers indicated the train's originating area: 5 was the code for the Exeter Division; 1 identified a Paddington down working; 6 a train from Plymouth or Cornwall. The codes changed annually.

They also served

R. C. Riley **13th July 1964**

While the Brunswick Green express engines swept by, humble, grimy tank engines shuffled about the adjacent sidings, junctions and marshalling yards; their duties as essential as they were unspectacular. This photograph of Westbury sidings shows 0-6-0 pannier tank no.4607, a representative of the largest class of GWR locomotives: the 5700 Class panniers, which numbered 863 engines. She is passing Westbury South signal box (closed in 1978) and taking the down main line to the west. The Salisbury lines diverge on her left hand side.

At the start of that year, only just over 300 members of this class were still in traffic. No.4607 was one of the last to go - in September 1965 - being cut up at Briton Ferry after a period in store at Westbury.

Westbury's importance was primarily as a junction: in the 1950's only one down West of England express stopped there and only three up, but there were good cross-country connections to Salisbury, Weymouth, Portsmouth, Bristol and Cardiff and push-pull trains worked in all directions from Westbury - to Warminster, Frome, Trowbridge and Patney & Chirton; and to connect with the main Bristol-Paddington line at Chippenham. Westbury shed was therefore a busy one, and in 1950 was home to 76 engines including a County and no fewer than sixteen Halls. It was sited just to the right of the scene shown here.

Pride of Old Oak

R. C. Riley **5th March 1960**

By way of contrast, this view shows Western traditions at their prestigious best. Old Oak Common shed has rostered two of its best-groomed engines to work Race Day Specials to Newbury Racecourse station. Castle No.5074 *Hampden*, newly arrived from Paddington, is leaving its train to turn on the turntable. Meanwhile, No.6010 *King Charles I* stands at the head of the Members First Class Special - the most prestigious of the Race Day workings and one of up to five specials which ran through non-stop from Paddington behind an immaculate top-link engine. The Members' train was normally a King turn and often included vintage ex-GWR stock with a dining car at each end. Other specials ran through from such diverse locations as Acton, Oxford, Cardiff and Taunton and the six platforms at Race Course station were busy indeed, at least on the dozen or so annual occasions when meetings were held.

In the box

H. G. Forsythe

A rare and interesting colour view inside a large manual signal box, taken by a far-sighted photographer who specialised in the human side of the steam railway. This is Reading West Main in 1963 when it was in the charge of Senior Signalman Blackall. It was one of the largest of its type on the Western Region, with some 280 levers.

Note the illuminated track diagrams above the levers which showed the area covered by the box and the train movements within it, and the shelf carrying the various block bells and indicators. The levers are colour-coded to indicate their function: red for stop signals, yellow for distants, black/white for placing detonators on the line and blue for activating electrically-operated points. Each lever carries a neat brass plate giving details of its function. The effort required to pull them varied considerably depending on how far from the box the signal or set of points was situated: signals could be anything up to a mile away but, even then, the operation of the lever was more a matter of technique than brute strength.

It is easy to forget the sheer size and complexity of the mechanical apparatus which once orchestrated the GWR's train movements. In 1922, for example, it included no fewer than 1,645 signal boxes; 594 ground frames; 21,600 signals; 9,200 independent discs; 11,310 points; 48,280 working levers; 1,298 level crossing gates; 29,289 long-burning lamps and 10,850 telephones.

The diesels arrive

H. G. Forsythe

Reading General in 1962. A Bristol-bound express waits for the starting signal to drop. The engine is No.7027 *Thornbury Castle* (now preserved at Tyseley) in ex-works condition but only a year or so from withdrawal. An unidentified Warship diesel-hydraulic is arriving with an eastbound express. Introduced in 1958, these ugly and short-lived machines had only a small edge over a well-handled Castle.

London bound

Derek Cross **July 1960**

Despite its unkempt appearance and a prominent steam leak, No.6844 *Penhydd Grange* is making brisk progress through Sonning Cutting with an up freight. This famous two mile section through Sonning Hill took the best efforts of 1,220 navvies to build in 1838-9 and a landslip there two years later caused the GWR's first serious accident, in which 8 passengers died.

Day of rest

R. C. Riley **16th August 1959**

This summer Sunday line-up of 0-6-0 pannier tanks at Old Oak Common shed includes three condensing engines headed by No.9700, so fitted for working the Metropolitan Line tunnels to the GWR depot at Smithfield Market. The scene is most unusual, main line locomotives normally standing this side of the coal stage - perhaps someone had blundered in sorting the grades of coal?

Fall from grace

R. C. Riley (above), J. C. Morgan

No.5042 *Winchester Castle* at Paddington: two photographs eloquently portraying the decline and fall of the steam locomotive. Above, in a picture taken on 20th June 1959, she approaches Westbourne Bridge signal box with the 1.45 pm Paddington-Worcester/ Hereford (correct reporting number 913). Her general cleanliness is typical of Worcester-based engines of the period.

Below: 31st May 1965, only eleven days before sister engine No.7029 *Clun Castle* took out Paddington's last public steam train, and No.5042, rostered to work the 16.15 departure, has fallen on hard times. Her fire still burns brightly but her time is nearly done. Stripped of name and number plates, her Brunswick Green livery obliterated with grime, she waits to leave Brunel's vaulted terminus for the last time. She was withdrawn a few days later.

Westbound stopper

Derek Cross **July 1960**

The entire GWR route between Paddington and Reading was four-track: down main, up main, down relief and up relief - with, in the 1950's, additional goods lines. Here, No.5994 *Roydon Hall* heads a Paddington-Swindon stopping train near Iver, where a standard-type GWR station was opened in 1924 to cater for increasing suburban traffic. It comprised a central island with two outer platforms, all surmounted with wooden buildings, and is still open today.

The intensity of traffic over this section prompted the GWR to install colour-light signalling between Paddington and Southall as far back as the early 1930's but it was to take another thirty years before it extended as far west as Iver.

Running-in turn

R. C. Riley **13th May 1961**

After heavy overhaul at Swindon Works, engines were despatched on running-in turns - usually local passenger - down to Bristol or up to Didcot and back. This is one such working - massive 128-ton Churchward Class 4700 2-8-0 No.4705 stands at Challow with the 10.25 am Didcot-Swindon, her fireman watching for the 'right-away'. The 47's were elusive engines for most of their forty years of existence, their primary role being the working of night express freights, but as early as the 1920's and well into the 1960's they were pressed into passenger service on West Country holiday expresses, a duty they performed admirably. In early 1961, No.4705 was a Laira engine, her eight sisters being divided between Old Oak, St Philip's Marsh and Southall sheds. The class was extinct by July 1964, Nos.4703/07 being the last in traffic.

Note Challow goods shed, its cavernous proportions evidence of its origins on Brunel's Great Western Paddington-Bristol main line, built to the noble broad gauge.

Coal from Wales

R. C. Riley **13th May 1961**

The little Faringdon branch left the Didcot-Swindon main line at the purpose-built junction station of Uffington which opened on 1st June 1864. Passenger traffic ceased early, on 31st December 1951, and Uffington's status was reduced to wayside station. It closed entirely on 7th December 1964 following withdrawal of remaining freight workings along the branch.

This view shows one of Churchward's handsome and successful heavy freight 2-8-0's, No.3805, running through Uffington with an up South Wales coal train, under the bridge built by the GWR in 1897 to replace a wide, unfenced level crossing on which several fatal accidents had occurred.

One of the 1939-built 2884 Class, No.3805 spent many years working out of South Wales' biggest shed: Newport (Ebbw Junction), whose allocation was dominated by 8-coupled tender and tank engines for hauling coal trains.

Passing the yard

M. Mensing **22nd September 1961**

Four months later and a few miles to the east, one of the ubiquitous Halls, No.6944 *Fledborough Hall*, was rattling a down freight through Moreton Cutting Yard, Didcot, which was constructed during World War II. Outshopped in September 1942 (and not named until 1947) she was one of the last of the 4900 series Halls, Hawksworth introducing a number of design improvements in the Modified Halls, commencing in March 1944 with No.6959.

6944

Strength....

R. C. Riley **15th August 1959**

Another of the 1939-built Class 2884 2-8-0's, No.3808, repainted ex-Swindon Works and probably on a running-in turn, photographed at Hinksey South heading a freight which terminated in the sidings south of Oxford.

....and character

R. C. Riley **20th April 1958**

Dukedog 4-4-0 No.9017 is seen at Oxford, taking water while working the Windsor-Cheltenham St James section of the Railway Enthusiast's Club 'Severn Rambler' rail tour. This engine was a March 1939 rebuild utilising the frames from Bulldog No.3425 and originally numbered 3217. Renumbered 9017 in 1946, she was withdrawn from Machynlleth shed in October 1960 - the last double-framed engine in regular traffic on BR. Subsequently purchased for preservation and with her original number restored, she is now a familiar sight on the Bluebell Railway.

Ready for the road

R. C. Riley **6th September 1959**

Newly overhauled and repainted Collett 4-6-0 No.5049 *Earl of Plymouth,* up from Newton Abbot shed, is readied for traffic outside Swindon's nine road 'straight' shed of 1871 vintage. The shed driver is oiling the Castle's right-hand outside valve spindle front end: he will oil right round the locomotive and use the pit to attend to those oiling points not otherwise accessible - and there were many of these on the GWR 4-cylinder 4-6-0's.

Interestingly, this engine cost £5,800 to build in 1936, £1,000 *less* than the pioneer batch of Castles of 1923-4 and No.5049, formerly *Denbigh Castle*, was one of twenty of her class to receive in 1937 the displaced nameplates of the 4-4-0's of the 3200 Class. She was fitted with a double chimney during the overhaul just completed, this improving her performance but doing nothing at all for her appearance.

Apart from the handful of rebuilds, the first 'pure' Castles were withdrawn that year, but it was another three years before scrapping of the class become large scale. No.5049 was withdrawn from St Philip's Marsh, Bristol, in March 1963 with a logged mileage of 1.28 million miles. While no Castle quite attained 2 million miles, many of the class were scrapped with less than one third of this total behind them: clear evidence that they were made prematurely redundant in the scramble for dieselisation.

The complete works

R. C. Riley **16th June 1957**

No.5911 *Guild Hall* is centre stage in this pageant of mechanisation inside 'A' Erecting Shop at Swindon Works, perhaps the GWR's most famous building, in which many of its most notable classes, including the Kings and Castles, were built. It replaced the old broad gauge shop in 1900 and its most impressive features were undoubtedly the massive overhead crane, which could lift a complete locomotive clear of its neighbouring engines and place it on the traverser and, at the eastern end, the engine testing plant (or 'home-trainer' as Swindon men dubbed it). This comprised a 'rolling road' test bed on which locomotives could be run at speeds equivalent to 70-80 mph while remaining stationary and connected to equipment measuring drawbar pull, water and coal consumption, etc.

Note, on the right, the preserved 8ft driving wheels of the 1851 broad gauge 4-2-2, *Lord of the Isles* (withdrawn in 1884 but not scrapped until 1906), which are now in Swindon Railway Museum.

King of the country

P. M. Alexander/Millbrook House Collection **Summer 1952**

Railway landscape photography at its

finest. Collett 4-6-0 No.6004 *King George III* lifts a featherweight Bristol-Swindon running-in turn towards Middle Hill Tunnel, situated just to the west of famous Box Tunnel and, at 198 yards, considerably shorter than its famous neighbour.

In the distance is Box station, which Brunel built on a lavish scale. The highly decorated single storey station building provided the inspiration for what was to become a GWR standard design. Box station closed on 4th January 1965 and little trace of it now survives.

No.6004 was one of the last of the Kings to be converted to double chimney - in August 1958 - but from 1955 this modification, in concert with increased superheat and re-draughting modifications to the smokebox, contributed to the Kings and Castles putting in the fastest speeds of their lives, notably on the accelerated 'Bristolian'. *King George III* ended her days in June 1962 at Cardiff Canton shed, which had received its first-ever allocation of the class in 1960 after the new diesel-hydraulics had displaced many 4-6-0's from the West of England expresses. She logged 1.91 million miles in her 35-year career, surely a good return on an investment of just £7,419.

Fading Star

P. M. Alexander/Millbrook House Collection **1952**

A rare colour photograph of one of the legendary Stars in action: No.4062 *Malmesbury Abbey* approaching Thingley Junction with the daily mixed passenger and milk tanks working from Swindon to Bristol. From about 1935 these 4-6-0's were progressively displaced from top link turns by Castles but even into the 1950's the survivors were often called upon to work heavy relief expresses.

Maid of all work

Derek Cross **July 1960**

The Stars' much more numerous cousins, the 330-strong Halls, evolved from the 2-cylinder Saints and the first, No.4900, was a rebuild of No.2925 *Saint Martin*, appearing in 1924. Here, No.4997 *Elton Hall* comes up the Avon Valley past milepost 105 at Bathampton with an eastbound freight.

Last of the line

P. M. Alexander/Millbrook House Collection **March 1962**

Last of the masterly line of GWR 4-6-0's, the Hawksworth Counties were built in two lots: Nos.1000-19 in 1945-46 and Nos.1020-29 in 1946-47. They represented the ultimate evolution of the Saint lineage of 2-cylinder 4-6-0's which embraced the Halls, Granges and Manors, and were the most powerful of all. Designed to meet post-war requirements for simplicity and ease of maintenance they were less sophisticated than their 4-cylinder stablemates but were useful machines and by the mid-1950's were handling the same type of work as the Castles.

Here, the photographer's viewpoint emphasises the squat, powerful aspect of the class as No.1017 *County of Hereford* emerges from the eastern portal of the Severn Tunnel with a Cardiff-Bristol train. The 4m628yd tunnel was opened in 1885. It had taken no less than twelve years to build - immense difficulties having been encountered - but saved 26 miles as compared with the route via Gloucester and greatly increased traffic along the Paddington-Bristol main line into South Wales. In steam days, ventilation was a particular problem and a powerful fan displacing 800,000 cubic feet of air per minute was installed.

Serving the port

Derek Cross **21st July 1963**

One of Southall's Granges, No.6841 *Marlas Grange*, takes water at Avonmouth Docks while working a RCTS tour of the Bristol and Gloucester areas. During the early 1900's the GWR expanded considerably its operations in the Avonmouth area to exploit the increasing freight tonnages anticipated at the new Royal Albert Dock. Two new routes to the port, via Pilning and Hallen Marsh Junction respectively, were opened and vast complexes of sidings developed: the interchange sidings at Holesmouth, for example, having forty roads.

At Avonmouth, the Port of Bristol Authority had its own fleet of steam locomotives, usually numbering about 30 and locally built by Fox Walker, Avonside or Peckett. By the date of this picture most had been replaced by diesels, the last going in August 1965. A survivor can be seen lurking behind the dock gate.

Tank engine turns

Geoffrey Bannister **August 1964**

An interesting main line turn was the pioneering railmotor service between Chalford and Stonehouse, which commenced on 12th October 1903 and survived right to the end of push-pull working on the Western Region in late 1964. For many years it was the preserve of 0-4-2 tanks of the 1400 Class, and here No.1474 waits at Stonehouse with a mid-morning Gloucester-Chalford train while sister engine No.1444 can be seen in the distance heading for Gloucester with the balancing working. No.1474 carries the long-superseded 'lion and wheel' emblem and an oil can nestling behind her splasher. Both engines were withdrawn from Gloucester (Horton Road) shed shortly afterwards - in November and December 1964 respectively.

Brunel's attractive matching stone shelters at Stonehouse were demolished in 1976 (despite being listed by the DofE) but the station remains open.

Scrap-yard bound

J. C. Morgan **27th March 1965**

Two scruffy engines on shed at Worcester: one of the big 6100 Class prairies, No.6155 (withdrawn seven months later) and No.6856 *Stowe Grange* (withdrawn that November and one of the last of her class in service). The latter engine is bereft of nameplates - removed for safe keeping, sold or stolen - and carries LMR overhead wire warning flashes.

Not one of the eighty Granges has been preserved, but nine Class 5100/6100 prairies have been saved while two still languish at Barry. The type was designed for suburban work but by the early 1960's had largely had made redundant by the flood of new DMU's.

Through the smoke

M. Mensing **16th May 1964**

Large prairie No.4124, one of the 5100 Class engines, is seen here banking an up part-fitted freight out of Ledbury Tunnel on the Hereford-Worcester line, which was 1323 yards long and bored on a 1 in 70 gradient. Most up freight trains needed banking and in this narrow, poorly ventilated single line tunnel conditions were thoroughly unpleasant for the banker's crew; noxious smoke and fumes from the train engine often forcing them to lie flat on the cab floor in an endeavour to find some unpolluted air. Up to 1960, Ledbury's own shed rostered engines for this odious duty but following its closure the bankers were Worcester-based, No.4124 being withdrawn from that shed in August 1964.

In this early morning view, the train engine is Modified Hall No.7910 *Hown Hall*. The banker is working bunker-first to minimise smoke nuisance for its crew in the tunnel. The track on the right is a level refuge siding ending in a sand drag to prevent runaways entering the tunnel; double track not recommencing until Ledbury North.

Dirt and grime

M. Mensing **15th May 1965**

Nostalgia sometimes makes us forget that the comparitive cleanliness of the steam railway in its more prosperous years was due entirely to unremitting graft by a huge staff of cleaners. During the financial stringencies of the 1960's, as cleaning staff became harder to find and to pay, the increasingly filthy condition of locomotives, rolling stock and stations alike graphically emphasised the steam railway's intrinsic dirt and grime.

Here No.6956 *Mottram Hall*, one of the wartime built engines, lays a thick smokescreen across the fields as, grinding up-grade with a southbound fitted freight, she takes the Wadborough line at Norton Junction near Worcester. Note the atomic flask on the leading wagon - an interesting contrast in energy techonology.

One of Gloucester (Horton Road)'s last remaining 4-6-0's, this engine is nearing the end of her days as steam is eliminated from the LMR. She was withdrawn five months later and cut up at Cashmore's Yard, Newport, in the summer of the following year. Delighted with the ease and cleanliness of working the new diesels, few enginemen would have mourned her passing: and even if the planners had not banished it, would the steam locomotive have survived the environmentalists?

Finale of the 4-6-0's

Brian Moone **5th October 1965**

Another 4-6-0 in its last days. Evening at Hartlebury and an empty oil tank train from Rowley Regis is storming through, bound for South Wales behind No.6815 *Frilford Grange*. She has only a few more weeks to go and was withdrawn the following month from Oxford shed, joining the melancholy processions of dead engines towed to the breakers' yards. Between 1957 and the end of British steam in August 1968, some 16,000 steam locomotives were taken out of service and their scrapping evolved into a lucrative industry: with copper prices at £500 a ton in 1965, a 2½-ton firebox, for example, was a valuable item.

Buttigiegs of Newport bid successfully for No.6815: by January 1966 she had ceased to exist.

Early morning local

Brian Moone **28th June 1965**

One of the last two steam-hauled services serving Kidderminster was the 7.59 am local passenger to Birmingham Snow Hill, photographed here between Kidderminster and Blakedown on a glorious summer morning. Class 4100 2-6-2T No.4168 lays a crisp exhaust into the early morning air while above a high-flying aircraft leaves a vapour trail. The engine has lost its smokebox and cabside number plates, handpainted versions having been substituted by Stourbridge shed. She worked her last train in September, one of the last survivors of the once numerous Great Western large prairies.

Running powers

Geoffrey Bannister **August 1964**

Between Shrewsbury and Welshpool, the single track main line was LNWR/GWR Joint, the Western having obtained running powers from the former company. Here, 4-6-0 No.7828 *Odney Manor* heads the 7.30 am Pwllheli-Shrewsbury (summer SO) just west of the site of Breidden station, which was closed to passengers on 12th September 1960. The Shrewsbury & Welshpool Joint climbs steadily at an average of 1 in 100 between Buttington Junction and Westbury (Salop) and includes stretches of 1 in 87 with a short length at 1 in 53, which the train is approaching. Up until the early 1960's, heavier loadings had necessitated the banking of many passenger trains between Welshpool and Westbury.

West Wales junction

P. M. Alexander/Millbrook House Collection **March 1962**

Activity at Whitland on the Newport-Fishguard main line. At right, one of the big Class 4200 tanks, No.4273, is passing through with an eastbound freight train from Fishguard and Milford Haven, most of the vans probably containing fish. Whitland became a junction in 1866 when the Tenby and Pembroke Dock branch opened, a train for which stands at platform 1 behind a prairie tank. This line is still open. From 1873 Whitland was also the transfer point for the rambling Cardigan branch (closed 1963) which diverged from the main line 2¼ miles further west, branch trains using platform 4 on the extreme right of the picture. In the left distance, a 4-6-0 is backing off Whitland shed, which was a somewhat ramshackle affair, latterly sub to Newport and closed in 1965. The modern station structures with lengthy, flat canopies date from 1958.

Evening of a Castle

P. M. Alexander/Millbrook House Collection **March 1962**

Carmarthen had the most important steam motive power depot in West Wales. It comprised a six-road 'straight' shed dating from 1906-7; repair shop and single-tip coal stage. A wide variety of classes were allocated: some 45 engines in 1950, including Moguls for the long run to Aberystwyth, Halls, prairie tanks and 1400 Class 0-4-2T's. Carmarthen also usually had a Castle or two for working its prestige turn - the Pembroke Coast Express - and this picture shows one of the most celebrated of that class turning on 87G's 65 foot turntable: No.5006 *Tregenna Castle*, with an unidentified sister engine behind.

Great Western driver J. W. Street, of 'I Drove the 'Cheltenham Flyer' fame, testified that No.5006 was 'the best engine for her work that I ever had'. Allocated to Carmarthen the previous September and here lit by a westering sun, she is prepared for an evening duty. She is just a few weeks from withdrawal.

New colours for old

P. M. Alexander/Millbrook House Collection **August 1961**

Variation in the livery of coaching stock provided one of the visual interests of Western Region train watching in the 1950's. Great Western revived chocolate and cream contrasted with the early BR 'blood and custard' and later maroon liveries, plus the occasional glimpse of Southern green on through workings. Here, the fireman of Oxford-based Modified Hall No.6970 *Whaddon Hall* has just started to fire his engine as she approaches King's Sutton with a down express composed of Southern stock.

Possessed in the 1950's by a wave of nostalgia, Swindon began applying lined Brunswick Green paint to almost every steamable locomotive, including those mixed traffic machines for which the standard livery had been lined black. In the case of the Halls, transformation commenced in mid-1955, along with the County 4-6-0's; the Granges and Manors following suit late in 1956.

Late summer of steam

M. Mensing **25th August 1962**

Later BR maroon livery and chocolate and cream stock are in evidence in this fine study of a latter-day Western express wending its way through the English countryside. It is 5.24 pm on a glorious late summer afternoon as No.7014 *Caerhays Castle* approaches Lakes Halt on the North Warwicks line with the 2.8 pm Weston-super-Mare -Wolverhampton Low Level. Behind the train the harvest is ready to be gathered in.

Before the diesels came

John Tarrant **18th October 1959**

A King at rest. No.6020 *King Henry IV* stands dead in the sun outside the 'straight' shed at Wolverhampton Stafford Road. Sunlight reflects on the great bulk of the boiler - which carried the double chimney noticably better, aesthetically, than the more graceful Castles - and emphasises the detailing of the bogie. This was to a complex pattern designed to keep the bogie wheels clear of the 16¼ inch diameter cylinders: it caused problems at various periods of the Kings' careers.

Stafford Road generally had an allocation of the class: 6 in 1932, 5 in 1938, 4 in 1947, 7 in 1950 and 6 in 1953. By 1960 the dominance of the diesel-hydraulics on West of England services had led to an increase in the number of Kings at the Midlands shed to a total of 11. No.6020 was a regular there for many years, leaving for the last time in July of 1962, the year that saw the demise of the entire class.

Main shed of the Wolverhampton Division, Stafford Road dated from the 1860's, marked the northern limit of the broad gauge, and was sited in a cramped position between the GWR and LMS main lines, a mile or so outside Wolverhampton Low Level. Its principal engines were passenger classes, freight locomotives being shedded at nearby Oxley.

Climbing the bank

M. Mensing **8th August 1964**

The late afternoon sun shines down on No.6871 *Bourton Grange* as she makes steady progress near the summit of Hatton Bank with a holiday Saturday south coast-Birmingham return working. The Grange class was originally intended to be much more extensive, but the Second World War curtailed the programme after eighty had been completed, No.6871 being outshopped in March 1939 and the last engine, *Overton Grange*, two months later.

In 1964, No.6871 was based at Oxley shed, from where she was withdrawn in October of the following year. The unbroken four-mile climb up from Warwick will have presented this sturdy 4-6-0 with few problems: one ex-GWR shed foreman remembers the Granges as 'the best engines the Western ever had.'

Work on the line

M. Mensing **8th October 1961**

Lapworth station was opened in 1855 (as Kingswood) and later transformed during the massive rebuilding programme on the GWR main line system which commenced at the turn of the century. Here, No.6029 *King Edward VIII* slows to a halt, preparatory to setting back onto the down line during Sunday single line working necessitated by PW work. The train is the 4.30 pm Wolverhampton Low Level-Paddington.

No.6029 was the last-built of the thirty Kings. Outshopped in August 1930, just over three years after the pioneer engine *King George V*, she carried the name *King Stephen* until May 1936 and in 1961 was an Old Oak Common engine, arriving there from Laira in July 1959. From their earliest days, the Kings were regulars on the Paddington-Birmingham main line, displacing the Stars on the heavy, 2-hour expresses.

Back from the coast

M. Mensing **5th August 1961**

Sunlight and shadow at the late, lamented station of Birmingham Snow Hill. Churchward Mogul No.7330 is arriving with the first part of a Barmouth/Aberystwyth/Birmingham relief.

As LMR electrification proceeded apace in the mid 1960's, it became clear that the GWR's line between Birmingham Snow Hill and Wolverhampton Low Level was under threat. A brief resurgence during 1965-6, when electrification work led to LMR services being diverted over the Western line, could not long postpone the inevitable and all express workings ceased on 4th March 1967. By the following March all services apart from local DMU's had been diverted away and in May 1969, astonishingly, Snow Hill was relegated to the status of unstaffed halt. It closed entirely on 6th March 1972 and, after lying derelict for some years, has now been swept away.

Parcels for Paddington

R. C. Riley **28th May 1960**

Wednesbury Central, a typical station on the GWR's route to the north-west. No.1004 *County of Somerset* heads the 8.55 am Birkenhead-Paddington parcels. This station closed on 6th March 1972, the neighbouring LNWR station eight years earlier.

A testing time

right

M. Mensing **20th September 1958**

The 11.45 am Birkenhead-Paddington has just passed West Bromwich station in the charge of another of Stafford Road's Kings, No.6001 *King Edward VII.* In 1953, this engine was subjected to intensive dynamometer car tests in connection with improved draughting modifications, during which she triumphantly handled 25-coach trains weighing nearly 800 tons.

The colour fades

M. Mensing **5th August 1961**

Waiting to leave. One of Machynlleth shed's Manors stands in Shrewsbury station at the head of the 3.50 pm to Aberystwyth, the brilliant sunlight draining the last vestiges of colour from her grimy paintwork. These handsome, lightweight engines arrived on ex-Cambrian metals in 1943, the first 4-6-0's to do so, and performed sterling service in Wales well into the 1960's. At 1960, West of England dieselisation had increased the Welsh allocation as follows: Oswestry (8), Machynlleth (6), Carmarthen (4) and Croes Newydd (1).

In 1952, various modifications to the smokebox of the engine seen here, No.7818 *Granville Manor*, led to similar alterations to the entire class, improving their steaming considerably.

The last hours

M. Mensing **27th July 1963**

In the 1980's, thanks to the dedication of a few, the Great Western enthusiast can enjoy a good cross section of preserved steam. Several key classes, though, are not represented.

This melancholy view, taken at Craven Arms shed, shows part of the withdrawn locomotive allocation from Shrewsbury: two of the now extinct County 4-6-0's - Nos.1017,1022 and 1026 were stored here - and a Mogul, probably No.7336.

For some eight months before their final, slow journey to Ward's Sheffield scrapyard these engines stood rusting at Craven Arms. Ripe for preservation, ready for a buyer. But the preservation movement had yet to gather strength and momentum. And nobody came.